Medvedev's Media Affairs

Courtship of the Russian News Media
from Flirtation to Breakup

By William Dunkerley

℗ **Omnicom Press**

Published by
Omnicom Press
New Britain, CT, USA
Publishers since 1981

www.OmnicomPress.com

Library of Congress Control Number: 2011936758
ISBN-10 0615527442
ISBN-13 9780615527444
Printed in the United States of America

This book is dedicated to the memory of Paul Klebnikov. His work in Russia exemplified the kind of consumer-centric journalism that is still so badly needed in the country today.

Preface

Starting with an account of an alleged
breakup, this book will take you back
through the drama of Dmitry Medvedev's
media affairs. You'll see how they got started
and where they've led.

But, understanding Russia's newspaper and
TV tribulations isn't easy.

For one thing the media are rather
dysfunctional in a way that is hard to
fathom. There's also a lot of misinformation
about the media floating around from those
who either lack solid first-hand knowledge
or who have some kind of ax to grind. None
of that facilitates getting a clear picture.

I set out to give an accurate account of the
media business and its dilemmas, covering
the period preceding the 2012 presidential
election. My knowledge and interpretation of

things is based on broad personal experience I've had with Russia's enigmatic media.

As a media business analyst and consultant, I've done intensive work in 17 different Russian cities. And, through my workshops and seminars, I've worked with hundreds of media managers, literally from Kaliningrad to Kamchatka.

In addition, I've advised government officials on ways to achieve press freedom and to create a healthy media sector. Some of my recommendations have been enacted into law.

The narrative of this book is intended to be easy to read and digest. I've included four contemporary reports that comment on the state of things at the times when they were written.

Although many of the perspectives expressed in the book have negative overtones, I can assure you that all is not hopeless.

The future for the Russian media is no doubt challenging. But Russia has a lot of very bright and talented media professionals. They have long struggled against very difficult odds, often with little success or reward. But their tenacity is remarkable. And therein lies the great potential for a better future.

W.D.
September 2011

Contents

Chapters

1. Love on the Rocks?   1
2. How It All Started   7
3. Enter Medvedev   15
4. Medvedev's Prime Initiatives   19
5   Russian Media Ethics 101   23
6. November 2009 Report   29
7. State-of-the-Nation 2010   35
8. December 2010 Report   39
9. The New Media Plan   45
10. January 2011 Report   49
11. The New, New Media Plan   57
12. July 2011 Report   61
13. Public Television   67
14. Conclusion   73
15. Appendix   81

Chapter 1
Love on the Rocks?

Dmitry Medvedev says it's time that the government and Russia's media part ways.

RUSSIAN President Dmitry Medvedev's love affair with his country's media is in the breakup phase. At least that's what he's been telling people lately.

He wants to end the attachment. That means going separate ways. Medvedev says he wants to get the government out of the media business.

That would be quite a big move. It's said that 80 percent of the country's media is controlled by some level of government. This would be practically the breakup of the century!

It's not that Medvedev no longer wants to see his name in print. ...or view his face on TV. All that's still good. He's willing to remain just friends.

What Medvedev longs for is financial freedom. He's not thinking of himself, mind you. This breakup is for the good of the media. The media have become too dependent. That's a problem.

They're not earning money on their own. They need to be supported. That's just not good for them. Not good for the country, either, he says.

But sometimes I think Medvedev is being coy about all this breakup talk.

You see, there are some outlets he wants to keep. They are the Moscow-based ones that have a national reach. When it comes down to brass tacks, he's not talking of putting them out on their own.

Instead, it's the far-flung media in the provinces that he's concerned about.

Why is he so focused on them? Those provincial outlets are being supported by governors and mayors and other politicians. Even business tycoons get into the act. This isn't money out of Medvedev's pocket. So what's his point?

Something's Mysterious

It's all a perplexing situation. It makes you wonder why someone has to support these media outlets in the first place. Why aren't they making money on their own?

In other developed countries lots of media outlets seem to be able to earn their own way without the help of some sugar daddy.

Why is Russia so different? What's wrong here? Is there a nefarious plot afoot?

Chapter 2
How It All Started

Why do Russia's media outlets need financial benefactors to support them?

MEDVEDEV isn't the father of all sugar daddies. He didn't start the system of big shots supporting media outlets.

It was present during the presidency of his predecessor, Vladimir Putin. Putin is often accused of clamping down on the free press that developed during the Yeltsin years.

That's all a lot of bunkum, though.

The sugar daddy system was in effect back in the 90s, too. In fact that's when it got its start. There weren't any truly independent media under Yeltsin. They were all conscripted by someone. Why, there wasn't any free press for Putin to have clamped down on!

There's No Free Press?

Why is that? Sometime early in Yeltsin's presidency, some really bad media laws were enacted. They made it practically impossible for media outlets to achieve financial success.

And without a way of supporting themselves, guess what? The media outlets had to find some way of surviving. That's where the sugar daddies came in.

Actually, calling them sugar daddies is somewhat of a misnomer. They were more than that. A better word for them is "overlords."

They called the shots. These media overlords put cash into the money-losing media outlets for one main reason: They wanted to color the news in their own favor. And they called that press freedom.

Free Press = Free to Lie

This all started on a basis of improvised corruption. If, say, a governor running for re-election wanted to boost his popularity, he could go to a newspaper and pay a fee. In return he'd get a nice article about him published in the newspaper.

Likewise, if a politician wanted to sponsor a journalistic hatchet job on a competitor, he could. Business tycoons also engaged in this pay-for-play as a means of advancing their business interests through the media.

Eventually, the country's political and business powerhouses wanted to formalize their control of the media.

The actions of Gazprom, the national gas monopoly, serve as an example. The company, which is controlled by the government, formed a subsidiary called Gazprom-Media. Its purpose was to manage Gazprom-controlled media outlets.

Gazprom-Media's chairman explained to *Kommersant* newspaper that the company wanted to legalize its "conjugal relations with certain mass media." To what end? The chairman explained that his company is "not indifferent as to who will govern the regions, who will pass laws, and what kind of government we will have." He added that Gazprom-Media will intervene in the editorial policy of the media outlets it partly owns or finances.

Gazprom was not alone in establishing a media empire. Business tycoons Vladimir Gusinsky and Boris Berezovsky each had their own, as did others.

Off to War

There came a time when opposing media empires engaged in what were called "information wars." In these battles of titans, media consumers were subjected to displays of disparate versions of the truth about what was happening in their country.

It's said that good journalism is the verbal equivalent of taking a picture to show others what you have seen. But, if one outlet says it saw a horse, and another says it saw a fish, while both of them were looking at a dog, the interests of the people are not being served.

And so it was – an abject failure of journalism.

A New War

Things changed when Vladimir Putin succeeded Yeltsin as president. He declared war on the dependency of media organizations upon political and commercial sponsors. In his first state of the nation address he said:

"But without a truly free press, Russian

democracy simply will not survive, and a civil society will not emerge. Unfortunately, we have not moved forward to draw up clear-cut democratic rules to guarantee the genuine independence of the 'fourth estate.' I want to underline that word 'genuine.' Meanwhile, however, journalistic freedom has become an irresistible temptation for the politicians and the largest financial groups to use the media as an instrument in inter-clan struggles. As the president of this country, I think it is my duty to draw the public's attention to this."

Moreover, beyond simply identifying the problem, he promised to change things. He said:

"Because of this, we must guarantee journalists genuine freedom, not just the pretense of freedom, by creating in this country the legal and economic conditions that are needed for civilized information businesses to exist."

In turn, Putin acted.

First, he chased Gusinsky and Berezovsky out of the country and took over their major media properties. The resulting government control was alleged to be only a temporary stewardship.

In addition, Putin repealed the bad media laws that had constrained media profitability. The Russian Media Fund, an American-Russian private sector initiative that I support, had successfully advocated for the changes in the laws.

But not much else changed.

Although the new laws made it possible for media companies to switch over to non-corrupt business practices, most of them didn't. The corrupt system of media finance had become entrenched.

And for the temporary stewardship of the taken-over media outlets? Well, it wasn't temporary, after all.

Woe be the poor Russian media consumer looking for honest news!

Chapter 3
Enter Medvedev

Who is Dmitry Medvedev, anyway?
How did his affairs with the media
get started?

DMITRY Medvedev succeeded Putin as president in 2008, after four years of stagnation in media reform. There had been a lot of activity during Putin's first term. But in the second four years the impetus for change seemed to have dissipated.

So it was with some surprise that media reform reappeared as an issue under Medvedev.

Medvedev and Putin had worked together during the early and mid-90s in the St. Petersburg city government. Medvedev was Putin's campaign manager in the 2000 presidential election. Afterward, Medvedev became chairman of Gazprom, the powerful natural gas monopoly.

Before entering politics, Medvedev had been a law professor at St. Petersburg State University.

Media reform has been far from Medvedev's top presidential objectives. Promoting modernization and fighting corruption have been his mainstays.

But a somewhat cryptic passage in his 2010 state-of-the-nation address hinted that media reform might be back on the table.

That one remark signaled the start of Medvedev's media affairs!

Chapter 4
Medvedev's Prime Initiatives

Modernization and de-corruption.

MEDVEDEV aspired to change society for the better. As he embarked upon his presidency, Medvedev began to champion two signature programs.

The first, modernization, was conceived to end Russia's heavy economic dependency on oil, natural gas, and other raw materials. Instead, Medvedev wanted to see an economic realignment with a focus on high-technology.

Targeted areas for development:

–space and telecommunications
–medical equipment and pharmaceuticals
–energy efficiency
–information technology
–nuclear technologies

Medvedev placed his hopes on developing a high-tech innovation center called Skolkovo. Certainly the exchange of reliable information in print or online should be an essential element of a national development project of this scale. But since even technical publications are subject to entrenched media corruption, it is hard to understand how these plans could have proceeded normally.

Medvedev's second prime initiative, curbing corruption, targets what many believe is the country's most pervasive problem.

In outlining his plan to deal with corruption, Medvedev reportedly said, "Corruption in our country has become rampant. It has become commonplace and characterizes the life of Russian society."

Medvedev set out to target corrupt government officials. New laws were enacted; many corrupt government officials and police were dealt with harshly. Even so, by January 2011, Medvedev was expressing disappointment. He said that officials were not coping well with the widespread corruption, and that the situation was "sad and dangerous."

But what about the country's most conspicuously corrupt sector of the economy: the media? What had been done there?

Chapter 5
Russian Media Ethics 101

What about the most conspicuously corrupt sector of the Russian economy?

WITH media corruption sticking out like a sore thumb, did Medvedev make it part of his original anti-corruption program? Sadly, he did not.

Meanwhile, media consumers were being cheated at every opportunity. They sought reliable news. But what they got was paid propaganda masquerading as news.

Did the media companies have a code of ethics?

The prevailing corrupt business practice could be summed up with the proverb "Kto platit, tot zakazivaet muziku," – He who pays calls the tune. That's the code. But where's the ethics? Where's the balance? Where's the fairness?

The media's financial overlords reigned supreme. This was a model for bad business behavior.

How did the media end up with this corrupt

business culture? ...one so devoid of ethical principles?

Were the media professionals fundamentally without principles right from the start? I don't think so. Instead, they were left with little alternative. The fault lies with the legal and economic framework, the bad laws.

The kind of position the media were put into is neither unique nor new. Indeed, at its heart, this is a kind of timeless problem. Dostoyevsky articulated it in the nineteenth century when he wrote, "Nakormi, togda i sprashivai s nikh dobrodeteli," – Feed men, and then ask of them virtue.

Has Nothing Changed?

It's still the same old story. News stories are bought and paid for in order to favor the business or political interests of the payer.

For media businesses there is no real opportunity for legitimate success. If you choose to be in the media business, you are choosing to be in the business of selling influence at the expense of your consumers' needs. Serving their needs and interests is not a priority. Few media companies could survive as honest, consumer-centric businesses.

These practices exist not only in the mass media, but in trade and professional offerings as well. Consumers are aware that they are being lied to by the media. And they don't like it. Indeed, multiple studies have shown that most Russians would prefer a return to official censorship over perpetuation of the present nonsense.

The legitimate media advertisers are negatively impacted, too. They advertise in order to reach prospective buyers. But, media audiences are aggregated to suit political exigencies instead of business needs. Pensioners are sought because they vote in disproportionately high numbers. That's good for the sponsors of distorted news. But pensioners are not big spenders. That's bad for the honest advertisers. As a result, media advertisers are unable to reach commercially active audiences efficiently. The consumer base is not being targeted.

None of this bodes well for Russia's economic outlook. Worldwide, media advertising is normally an engine of commerce. It brings together buyers and sellers. But when the consumer base is not targeted in media audience aggregation, there is a systemic breakdown. It retards commerce in all sectors of the economy. It is inimical to economic growth and development.

Shouldn't Medvedev have been doing something about all this?

Chapter 6

November 2009 Report

Modernization ... corruption ... and the media. What should Medvedev do about them? Step 1: Get the government out of the media business!

PRESIDENT Dmitry Medvedev should start his modernization program by taking a hard look at the sorrowful state of the media in the country.

Russia's media are awash in a corrupt culture of paid-for news stories — propaganda masquerading as news. Few news outlets are free to tell the whole truth. Instead, they are subjugated by those who put money into the loss-making media companies in return for an opportunity to color the news in their own favor. They constitute a pluralistic but conscripted press, hardly a free press.

Articles are paid for not only by businesspeople, but by mayors, governors, and natural resource monopolies controlled by the state. The government is clearly a big part of the problem.

With little free press, it is difficult for the electorate to make informed choices during elections, and the people are deprived of the aid of a Fourth Estate in exercising vigilance over their government.

Medvedev says he wants to make developing information technology a national priority. But without first normalizing the media sector, that sparkling new technology may succumb to the old garbage-in, garbage-out phenomenon.

Medvedev also says he wants to institute zero tolerance for corruption. Yet he seems willing to leave the nation's most conspicuous center of corruption — the media — to continue with business as usual.

It's hard to imagine that Medvedev's hope for a better Russia will ever be realized if he doesn't address the issue of media corruption. I'd like to offer him a simple, two-step prescription for turning things around:

Step 1:

Get the government out of the media business. It may be debatable whether there is anything fundamentally wrong with government media ownership. Nonetheless, it looks bad and plays into the hands of those who use it to tarnish Russia's image internationally. Government ownership in the media sector sends an ominous signal, as well, to legitimate entrepreneurs who might like to get into the media business. The government's role in the well-documented corrupt business culture that dominates the media also casts a dark shadow upon Medvedev's vision of a less corrupt future for Russia.

Step 2:

Clean up the other corruption in the media. When a consumer buys a bag of potatoes, he doesn't want to find that the bag is also full of garbage. Similarly, when Russians watch news broadcasts, they deserve not to have the news intermixed with disguised propaganda.

In reality, the disguise isn't fooling anyone. Any Russian can spot phony news. Not only do Russians recognize paid-for news stories. They also despise them. They know that the media are not serving the needs and interests of the people.

Many Russians have been quietly irate over this for years. They would rather see a return to censorship than a continuation of the current nonsense. That would seem to be an important mandate for change. And clearly cleaning up the corruption would be a more productive choice than reimposing censorship. The Russian Media Fund has even developed a plan that the administration can use to bring about the change.

It's Time to Get Serious

Paid-for news content makes Russia's media a megaphone for corruption. Kicking off an anti-corruption campaign with the media sector will touch every citizen and every segment of commerce.

That would be a strong start.

Chapter 7
State of the Nation 2010

Here comes the media bombshell –
and it's actually good news!

BURIED in a litany of other priorities in Medvedev's state-of-the-nation address came the line, "The government authorities should not own factories, newspapers, or ships."

That was it. This was the start of Medvedev's impending breakup with the media.

News coverage of his address focused on other issues. Topics like:

–nuclear arms
–fighting corruption
–police reform
–economic problems
–trouble with Georgia
–social issues

Nonetheless, his cryptic media-related comment stood out: "The government authorities should not own ... newspapers...!" Did he really mean it? And if so, what did he really mean? It was a mystery, yet a cause for hope.

Chapter 8
December 2010 Report

The big news from Medvedev's address to the nation is that he has come around to Step 1 (see Chapter 6). He says he actually wants to get the government out of the media business!

"DMITRY Medvedev, emancipator of Russia's media." That may well be how the current president will go down in history. In this year's state-of-the-nation address, he signaled that the government would begin selling off its extensive media holdings. That's a good, indeed a bold move toward unshackling Russia's subjugated press.

The government in Russia has occupied too much of the media landscape for too long. But the subjugation extends far beyond the Kremlin walls. Governors, mayors, and other political figures are engaged in media ownership and control throughout all Russia. I hope that Medvedev's vision for getting the government out of the media business will consider them, too.

Medvedev's media initiative will be no easy task, however. Russia's media sector has been a dysfunctional mess for decades. It's not just the government; it's the business tycoons, too. All these media overlords want to color the news in their own favor and make their competitors look bad. Consumer needs and interests take a backseat.

An Enigmatic Situation

Westerners find it hard to understand how things got so bad. For the past decade, Vladimir Putin has been a scapegoat. The story goes that he tyrannically clamped down on Russia's free press. Closer examination reveals, however, that there never was a free press to begin with.

From the beginning of the Russian Federation, laws were imposed that made media business profitability quite elusive. To stay afloat, enterprising media managers formed corrupt alliances with politicians and businessmen. The deal was that those folks would put money into the loss-making media ventures so they could call the shots. As one headline put it, "The Best News Rubles Can Buy."

That's still the deal today. Putin repealed the constraining laws in his first term as president. But the corrupt practices had become entrenched and still remain. Now Medvedev just may be able to change all that. "It's a waste of money," Kremlin economic adviser Arkady Dvorkovich said of today's governmental media ownership. That's quite an understatement. All the media shenanigans haven't fooled Russian consumers. Surveys show that they know they're being fed a phony bill of goods. So the government has been spending money to lie to people who know they're being lied to. That's quite a waste.

Dvorkovich went on to say, "It will not do us any good if [the media outlets] fall into the hands of dishonest investors." But keeping all of the media above board may not be realistic. The important thing is to get at least one consumer-centric media outlet in each major media market. Consumers will recognize who's there to serve their interests, and who's not.

Market forces will put the phonies in their place. On top of that, the Russian Media Fund has a ready-made plan to diminish the role of paid-for news in Russian society. Medvedev should check it out.

And while a government media pullout can't happen overnight, time is of the essence. Ambitious plans are afoot for modernization, anti-corruption, forward-looking projects like Skolkovo, and new social programs. Their chances of success would be enhanced if Russia were to have a normalized, consumer-centric media industry. But for now, the media constitute the nation's most conspicuously corrupt economic sector.

Shouldn't that propel Medvedev's media initiative to the level of a categorical imperative?

Chapter 9
The New Media Plan

What's in the plan? How will its goals be achieved?

AS clarifications began to emerge on exactly what Medvedev's new media initiative would entail, questions started to arise about whether it is a sensible plan.

There seems to be a lot of emphasis on selling off media outlets that are owned by provincial politicians. But, is that practical? And will it have much of an impact?

If selling off the media outlets in the provinces is a good idea, why wouldn't it also be wise to set loose the national outlets based in Moscow? Why isn't that part of the plan?

Shouldn't the idea of getting the government out of the media business apply to all levels of government?

Unfortunately these questions seemed to cast doubts on the clarity of purpose behind Medvedev's media plan.

Would everyone's hopes for a better media

future just go down the drain?

Chapter 10

January 2011 Report

There's a flaw in the new media plan!

IS the Russian government trying to cash in on the sale of worthless media properties?

President Dmitry Medvedev has announced plans to divest the state of its assorted media holdings. But, what's a Russian media outlet worth? *Newsweek* magazine sold for just $1 last year. I wonder how much the Russian outlets will bring in.

Some insiders may already be anticipating a bonanza from the mass sell-off. But before too many visions of rubles dance in their heads, it's worth asking whether all these media companies have any real commercial value.

Since the start of the Russian Federation, I've worked with media companies from all over Russia. I've analyzed client companies and their competition. In all candor, it's rare to find a profitable indigenous media company. More commonly, a business with an inadequate audience and advertising revenues will sell propaganda that masquerades as news to compensate for the revenue shortfall. Who's going to buy into such a corrupt, dirty business?

Presidential economic advisor Arkady Dvorkovich said he'd like to keep the sold-off media companies out of the hands of "dishonest investors." I'd like to know how he's going to do that!

The purpose of a commercial enterprise is to produce profits. Given that, what's the value of one that produces losses?

Newsweek was put up for sale by The Washington Post Company because the publication was incurring losses. But before last year's sale, *Newsweek* made a valiant effort to rehabilitate itself. Managers changed the audience makeup, did a graphic redesign and editorial repositioning, and attempted to boost revenues.

But in the process they made serious mistakes in judgment. Maybe the magazine's new owner will have a better go at it.

Can the state-controlled, unprofitable media companies in Russia be rehabilitated? Can they become legitimate businesses that will attract "honest investors"?

Some circumstances will prevent that. First, there are too many media companies in Russia — more than the economy could support as legitimate businesses. Second, the media field generally has a deficit of business acumen. And finally, the ingrained corrupt culture of paid-for news would be a difficult institution to eradicate.

A Nefarious Plot?

On top of that, there is the question of whether the government really wants to get out of the media business. Some predict that the media outlets will end up being acquired by friends or supporters of the current political owners.

Others suggest that the entire sell-off is just a ruse to wrest control of the outlets from regional leaders and put them under the power vertical. Legislating "subsidies" to aid the "transition away from government ownership" seems consistent with that supposed scheme.

I strongly support Medvedev's initiative to get the government out of the media business. He's right: It doesn't belong there. In his televised December interview, he asserted that news decisions should be made independently of governmental influence. Right again.

But how's that going to be accomplished? This isn't a simple matter. It doesn't seem practical to assure absolute transparency of ownership or to know the allegiances of the new owners. What's more, it is hard to define what a governmentally owned outlet is. The owner of record may appear to be an independent company, but the beneficial owner may be a politician or state entity.

What's a beneficial owner? Take this example: A city mayor induces companies to advertise in a particular newspaper, even if they have no products to sell the readers. In return, those companies are favored by the mayor. Out of gratitude to the mayor, the newspaper supports him and diminishes his opponents. Without the advertising revenues the mayor brought in, the paper wouldn't be able to pay its bills.

Who's the beneficial owner of this media company? I say it's the mayor.

So, not only does it seem impossible to keep sold-off media properties from operating under covert state control, but it's not even possible to identify which media companies are currently under governmental control!

What a mess! Why bother trying to sell the media companies? Instead, why not identify those that are not operating profitably and that rely upon selling phony news stories? These companies should be closed, not sold. Just put a stop to the nonsense.

Closing the Failed Outlets

Should a government be doing the shuttering? Of course not. Medvedev is finally seeking to reduce the state's heavy-handedness with the news media, not to increase it.

Closing down those hack media outlets is something that consumers can do. All they need are some good media outlets to choose from. That's where the administration's focus should be. It must create the conditions for truly consumer-centric media outlets to emerge and thrive. Those will be the outlets of consumer choice. The existing crop of self-censoring, ax-grinding purveyors of dishonest news will be put in their place and marginalized, if not closed completely.

And the original plan to sell the governmental media outlets? I'm reminded of the Russian proverb, "Pivo bez vodky, dengi na veter," – Beer without vodka is money thrown to the wind. Perhaps the same could be said about a media enterprise without profits.

It's just not a smart idea to try selling it.

Chapter 11
The New, New Media Plan

What's new about the new plan?

NOW a public TV proposal has been added. That's good. But isn't it time for us to see some results?

Many of us had high hopes for Medvedev's media initiative. It held promise for reforming many long-standing problems with the media. And in turn, that would help ameliorate a lot of the seemingly intractable problems throughout Russian society.

For some, dashed hopes seem to be a perennial problem in Russia.

One-time Yeltsin prime minister Victor Chernomyrdin said famously about the 1990s economic transition to capitalism, "Khoteli kak luchshe, no poluchiloc' kak vsegda," – We wanted something better, but just got more of the same.

Is that what the Russian media is in store for – just more of the same?

Chapter 12
July 2011 Report

Maybe Medvedev should try leading by example!

"DO as I say, not as I do!"

Is that what President Dmitry Medvedev is telling us about his new media plan? He released the new proposals at a meeting of the St. Petersburg Dialogue held July 19 in Hannover, Germany. The plan is to get the government out of the media business, and create a public television channel.

Medvedev especially wants to get rid of regional government media bosses. But what about the Kremlin-controlled media based in Moscow? If the president truly wants the government out of the media business, why doesn't he lead by example? The Kremlin-tethered outlets should be the first ones to go.

Medvedev explained to his audience, "...if media sources [in the regions] receive money from the regional leadership, they start to serve its interests and turn into a mouthpiece for one person or several people."

His description is spot on. Paradoxically, when it comes to the Kremlin-controlled media, Medvedev is mum. Haven't those outlets turned into mouthpieces, too?

Medvedev, however, seems fixated on the regional media. "It would be a lot better if they existed independently," he told the Hannover gathering. Isn't the same true of the national media that are tied to the Kremlin?

Déjà Vu

Medvedev's new plan sounds a lot like his old media plan, which he presented during his state-of-the-nation address last November. Basically, the plan was to get the government out of the media business. But the government is still in there. The plan appears to have failed.

His new plan is essentially the same as his old one except for the addition of the public television proposal. The original plan was basically good. The new plan with its public TV component is even better.

Medvedev is great at making plans, but now he should concentrate on making sure that they bear fruit.

Here's my suggestion: Medvedev should set free the Gazprom-Media properties. Before becoming president, Medvedev was one of the very media overlords he now disdains. As chairman of Gazprom, he held ultimate control of Gazprom-Media, owner of a flock of major broadcast and print outlets.

Now, he should break up that media group. Sell off the individual properties. Be sure that they don't end up in politically-connected hands.

This won't be easy. Neither will the eradication of political control over the regional media. However, breaking up Gazprom-Media is something that Medvedev can initiate tomorrow. It would be a giant step in the right direction. It would demonstrate clearly that he's capable of producing more than just compelling ideas.

It would be an example of strong leadership by example.

Chapter 13
Public Television

A possible step in the right direction. But, can it be accomplished with honest intent?

PUBLIC television could play a positive role in Russia's distancing itself from the current corrupt media milieu. That is, if it can be instituted without the conscripting financial strings that plague the existing media offerings. Indeed, that's what Medvedev says he has in mind with his proposal. No strings attached.

The only problem with public TV, in his mind, is how to pay for it. But isn't that the problem all Russian media outlets faced right from the beginning? The methods of finance have left the consumers without news products that serve their needs and interests.

Not a New Idea

The idea of public television for Russia is not new.

Indeed, Russia had public TV during the 90s. It was created by a presidential decree of Boris Yeltsin in November 1994. The channel was called "Obshchestvennoe Rossiyskoye Televidenie," ORT, i.e., Russian Public Television.

Controlling ownership (51 percent) was held by government agencies. The balance was in private hands.

ORT carried Russia's most popular talk show. It was hosted by Vlad Listiev, who also was appointed director of the channel. He was unable to serve for long, though. Tragically, he was murdered in March 1995. His murder was never solved.

Public Became Private

At some point Boris Berezovsky, the business tycoon, managed to take control of the channel. It has been reported that he used ORT to promote the re-election of Yeltsin in 1996. Yeltsin had entered the election season with an approval rating of only about 5 percent.

Later, during Putin's first term as president, control of ORT was wrested away from Berezovsky. The channel then began operating under the ownership of the All-Russia State Television and Radio

Broadcasting Company as "Channel One." So the channel has gone from public to private to state.

What's Ahead?

Speaking about his new public TV proposal while in Hannover, Medvedev said, "If we are to build public television, we need to clearly answer the question of what money will be used to develop it."

That's really the central question. How it is answered will determine whether or not public television can be instituted in Russia with transparent and honest intent.

Chapter 14
Conclusion

What does this all add up to?

ULTIMATELY Dmitry Medvedev's media affairs involve two fundamental concepts that are vital to Russia's democratic and economic development. They are press freedom and a healthy media sector. Russia badly needs them both – but in a real sense has neither.

Freedom of the press is an implicit and essential right of the people. It is not just freedom of speech for journalists. If a democracy is going to work, citizens have got to make informed political choices. The media are the people's primary means for keeping informed.

Many believe that press freedom exists if the media are free of governmental control and that pluralism prevails. That view misses the main point. A good share of the media has got to be free to serve the people.

Why hasn't Russia been able to achieve this? I've shown in this book how propaganda masquerading as news is so prevalent in

Russia. It is paid for by oligarchs and other business concerns, by mayors, governors, and other politicians, and even by natural resource monopolies controlled by the presidential administration. They've conscripted media outlets to advance their own interests. That's the main problem.

Is it possible that the press could be both subjugated and free at the same time? Of course not. That is oxymoronic.

Someone once said that with freedom of the press, the people own the news. It's not owned by the government, or by the powerful elite. But, in Russia, most of the media are beholden to financial overlords. They own the news. That's a tragedy.

Russian consumers are so outraged over the state of the media that most have favored imposing censorship to end the nonsense. The level of dissatisfaction has reached as high as 76 percent. There is little doubt that the current media sector is an abomination in consumer terms.

If the news is to serve the people, the people have got to pay for the news. Then, they will own the news. But if they were to pay the full cost, it would probably be ten times the present price of a subscription. People aren't going to pay that. For most of the world, that's why we've got advertising in publications, print or online, and in broadcasting. Indeed, in the West, for example, almost 60% of newspaper content is advertising.

Post-communist countries that have made the greatest strides in press freedom are ones where the commercial success of the media is assured by sufficient advertising. I mean legitimate advertising, not phony, paid-for stories.

But most Russian media outlets remain mired in corrupt alliances with financial overlords. As a result, there is little value placed on developing consumer-responsive news and information products.

Pity the unfortunate readers and viewers. Pity also the advertisers! They are getting shortchanged by the current system, too. The people who pay to distort the news want to reach voters. Advertisers need to reach buyers. Too large a percentage of the population lacks the financial means to buy much that is advertised. Pensioners have perhaps the lowest disposable income. But, they have a high propensity to vote. Media outlets actively seek them as readers, viewers, or listeners. The consumer base is less important politically.

If things are to change, the paid-for news stories have got to go. To me, the persistence of this system is actually astonishing. It embodies an enormous cognitive disconnect. It is the idea that misleading the people is a good way of influencing them, even though the people know they are being misled.

I realize that my commentary may sound quite negative. But, actually, I believe that the Russian media market now offers enormous promise.

Russia itself has a lot of very capable, intelligent, and honest media managers and journalists. Some of them have been successful in choosing a path away from the current corrupt system. But not enough of them. Not enough to move the entire media industry in a different direction.

The growth of press freedom and a healthy media sector in Russia depends on these people to reject the status quo. But the specter of change can be forbidding. I hope that more will find the courage and strength to choose a new course, a free course. Medvedev should pave the way with strong leadership. Then his media affairs could produce substantive results, not just talk.

Appendix

About the Author

William Dunkerley is a media business analyst and consultant specializing in Russia and other post-communist countries. He has written extensively for *Sreda*, Russia's first media management magazine, and for *The Moscow Times*.

Mr. Dunkerley has been a featured speaker at media business conferences in seven post-communist countries, including the World Congresses of the International Federation of Journalists and the World Association of Newspapers.

He is principal of William Dunkerley Publishing Consultants, and editor and publisher of two industry publications: *Editors Only* and the *STRAT Newsletter*.

The Russian Media Fund

The Russian Media Fund, mentioned several times in this book, is a project backed by the International Center for Journalists, the Russian Media Research Center Sreda, and William Dunkerley Publishing Consultants. RMF requested and received a formal invitation from the Putin administration to offer advice on reforming the media sector. Since then, it has successfully advocated for changing the media regulatory structure. As a result, it has become technically possible for a media company to operate successfully without a need for corrupted revenues.

Omnicom Press

Omnicom Press, publisher of this book, was founded in 1981 to offer publishing products and printing services. It now offers print-on-demand books and e-books. The e-books can be read on PCs, laptops, notebooks, tablets, e-readers, and smartphones.

www.ingramcontent.com/pod-product-compliance
Lightning Source LLC
Chambersburg PA
CBHW060636210326
41520CB00010B/1628